BIBLE THEMES

*A unique approach to critical themes in the Bible
designed for individual and group study*

VALLI KANE

WESTBOW
PRESS®
A DIVISION OF THOMAS NELSON
& ZONDERVAN

WestBow Press books may be ordered through booksellers or by contacting:

WestBow Press
A Division of Thomas Nelson & Zondervan
1663 Liberty Drive
Bloomington, IN 47403
www.westbowpress.com
844-714-3454

ISBN: 978-1-6642-3056-9 (sc)
ISBN: 978-1-6642-3055-2 (e)

Library of Congress Control Number: 2021907222

Print information available on the last page.

WestBow Press rev. date: 08/23/2021

MESSAGE FROM
THE AUTHOR

Can the Bible be condensed? Is there a *Reader's Digest* version? I certainly would never espouse such a thing, but a single thread keeps going through my mind. God has created a path for us to follow in order to find peace in our earthly lives and for us to live with him in his eternal kingdom. Moreover, he has offered us the opportunity to walk it by his grace, if we believe in the death and resurrection of his son, Jesus Christ. He is so good. Who can conceive of a love so great?

The following are but some of the themes that travel from one end of the Bible to the other. Provided with each theme is a list of scripture verses, by no means exhaustive, that enlighten the theme and will inspire interesting study and conversation.

Notice that there are few explanations provided in this Bible study. The goal, and I hope the pleasure, is that you will dig into the scriptures yourself and experience the presence of God as he speaks directly to you.

Blessings,
Valli Kane

CONTENTS

HEAVENS

Everything in creation plays a role in revealing the nature of God. The Bible tell us exactly how the heavens make him known to the entire world.

Psalm 19:1–4
Psalm 50:6
Psalm 89:5
Psalm 96:11
Psalm 97:6
Psalm 119:89
Luke 21:25
Romans 1:20

YOUR THOUGHTS

GOD IS A JUST GOD

While justice must be served, our holy God does provide the means to restore our relationship with him and enjoy being in his presence.

Job 34:12
Psalm 89:14, 99:4, 8
Proverbs 6:23
Ecclesiastes 3:17
Jeremiah 18:1–10
Ezekiel 16:42, 39:21–29
Romans 2:9–11, 3:21–26
Colossians 2:13–14
Hebrews 2:1–3, 7:22–28
Revelation 16:7

YOUR THOUGHTS

_____
_____
_____
_____
_____
_____
_____
_____
_____
_____
_____
_____
_____
_____
_____
_____
_____
_____
_____
_____
_____
_____
_____
_____
_____
_____
_____
_____

GOD'S ANGER/CUP/BOWL

God pours out his wrath, as described throughout the Bible. Jesus asked, "Can you drink the cup I am going to drink?" (Matthew 20:22). Just imagine.

Psalm 75:7–10
Isaiah 51:17–23
Jeremiah 7:20, 25:15–38
Obadiah 1:15–16
Matthew 20:20–22
Revelation 14:9–11, 15:5–16:1

YOUR THOUGHTS

_____

_____

_____

_____

_____

_____

_____

_____

_____

_____

_____

_____

_____

_____

_____

_____

_____

_____

_____

_____

_____

_____

_____

WE ALL SIN

Paul ran the race for the kingdom of God. "We All Sin" was painted across the starting line (Romans 3:23). We all have to start our faith journey somewhere, and that is the place!

Genesis 6:5, 8:21
Psalm 143:2
Isaiah 64:6
Micah 7:4
Romans 3:23, 7:14–8:4
1 Corinthians 6:11
Ephesians 2:1–10

YOUR THOUGHTS

MAKE A PATH

God will lead us. Are we willing to follow him?

Psalm 77:19, 85:13, 105:17, 107:4–9
Isaiah 40:3–5, 43:15–21
Luke 1:76–79, 3:4–6
John 1:23, 14:6
1 Thessalonians 3:11

YOUR THOUGHTS

MAKING A DECISION FOR CHRIST/ ACCEPTING THE GIFT

God hates sin. In the Old Testament, God wants people to choose (Deuteronomy 30:19–20) to be good, to "reason together" with him. He wants them to be "willing and obedient." Unfortunately, this willingness to obey doesn't get the most righteous of us to "eat the best from the land" because it just never lasts (Isaiah 1:18–20). In the New Testament, God's offer of salvation requires a choice also if we are to enter God's best place. We are to choose to accept Jesus Christ as our Lord and Savior and allow the Holy Spirit to indwell us, live in us, and help us to live in God's will more every day. Jesus is a gentleman. He will not break down the door of your heart. He stands at the door and knocks (Revelation 3:20). It is your choice whether you will open the door and invite him in, *and it is never too late!*

Deuteronomy 30:19–20
Joshua 24:14–15
2 Chronicles 15:12–13
Isaiah 1:18–20
Jeremiah 11:1–5, 21:8, 29:13
Mark 10:13–16
Luke 14:15–24, 23:39–43
John 1:10–13
Acts 10:43–48
Romans 10:9–13
2 Corinthians 6:1–2
Revelation 3:20

YOUR THOUGHTS

BELIEVING BY FAITH, NOT BY SIGHT

God's truth is seen by our spirit, not our eyes.

Numbers 14:20–23
Joshua 1:16–17
Psalm 77:19
Jonah 2:8
Habakkuk 2:2–4
Luke 5:5
Romans 1:17, 4:18
1 Corinthians 2:6–16
2 Corinthians 4:18, 5:5–7
Galatians 3:11
Hebrews 10:38–39, 11:3, 13

YOUR THOUGHTS

TO BE "IN CHRIST"

To be connected with Christ at the soul level is a complicated concept, but don't let that scare you. He wants to be one with you and has created the means for that to happen. Nourish your "mustard seed of faith" (Matthew 17:20), and your experience of being "in Christ" (2 Corinthians 5:17) will slowly grow and blossom.

Psalm 90:1
John 14:8–14
2 Corinthians 5:16–21
2 Timothy 2:11–13

YOUR THOUGHTS

FISHES AND LOAVES/
MUSTARD SEED/
SEED OF FAITH

God multiplies what we offer him in blessings—sometimes to ourselves and sometimes to others.

1 Kings 17:8–16
2 Kings 4:1–7, 42–44
Matthew 14:13–21, 15:32–38, 17:20

YOUR THOUGHTS

_____

_____

_____

_____

_____

_____

_____

_____

_____

_____

_____

_____

_____

_____

_____

_____

_____

_____

_____

_____

_____

_____

_____

LIVING WATER

Water is necessary for physical life for the earth and all who dwell upon it. "Living water" (Matthew 4:10) is water that gives us internal life. It washes away our pain as well as our sins. It cleanses us in a way physical water cannot and is a gift from our Lord, Jesus Christ, when we accept deep down the reality of who he is.

Psalm 36:8–9
Isaiah 12:3
Zechariah 13:1, 14:8–9
John 4:7–14, 7:37–39
Revelation 22:1–2

YOUR THOUGHTS

BEING TRANSFORMED
INTO A NEW CREATION

God can change us into the people we are meant to be.

Romans 12:1–2
2 Corinthians 3:18, 4:16–18, 5:16–21
Galatians 6:15
Ephesians 4:20–24
Colossians 3:5–14

YOUR THOUGHTS

_____

_____

_____

_____

_____

_____

_____

_____

_____

_____

_____

_____

_____

_____

_____

_____

_____

_____

_____

_____

GROWING INTO THE PEOPLE WE ARE INTENDED TO BE IS A PROCESS

When we accept Christ as our Lord and Savior, the Holy Spirit will come to dwell inside of us and help us to live more like Christ every day. We must be cautious, however, not to judge ourselves or others harshly, as we will always be a work in progress and never reach the perfection of our Lord. Having said that, rejoice in the small and large victories you will see in yourself and others. As they say, "God is not finished with me yet!"

Psalm 40:3
Ezekiel 18:30–32
Hosea 10:12
Micah 6:8
John 3:30
Romans 12:1–2
2 Corinthians 3:18, 4:6–7, 16–18
Ephesians 4:14–16, 20–24
Philippians 1:6–11, 3:12–16
1 Thessalonians 2:13, 3:13
2 Peter 1:3–9

YOUR THOUGHTS

_____

_____

_____

_____

_____

_____

_____

_____

_____

_____

_____

_____

_____

_____

_____

_____

_____

_____

_____

_____

_____

_____

_____

GLASS DARKLY, SHADOW/ REALITY, MYSTERY

We see glimpses of the kingdom of God once we believe. The longer we are in relationship with Christ, the clearer our vision of God's kingdom becomes. We need to cling to this when we have unanswered prayers. Only God knows the big picture and the future.

Deuteronomy 29:2–4
Job 26:14
Ecclesiastes 8:16–17
Luke 24:30–32, 45
John 12:16
1 Corinthians 2:6–10, 4:1–5, 3:9–12
Ephesians 3:1–13
Colossians 2:17
Hebrews 10:1
1 John 3:2

YOUR THOUGHTS

_____

_____

_____

_____

_____

_____

_____

_____

_____

_____

_____

_____

_____

_____

_____

_____

_____

_____

_____

_____

_____

_____

_____

_____

TAKING OFF/PUTTING ON: DYING TO SELF

This expression does not mean we cease to be ourselves (John 3:3). When we surrender our lives to Jesus, we exchange our natural inclinations for his supernatural inclinations in an ever so slowly but consistent way through the power of the Holy Spirit. The promise is that we take off our sinful clothing and put on his clothing of righteousness, which will fit better and better the longer we walk this life hand in hand with him. The hope we have of our existence in heaven is even more beautiful and comforting than that, for there our heavenly robes will fit just right!

Matthew 10:37–39, 16:25
John 3:30
Romans 6:1–8, 7:4–6, 21–25
2 Corinthians 4:10–12, 5:1–5, 17
Galatians 2:19–21, 5:16–24, 6:15
Ephesians 4:20–24
Philippians 3:20–21
Colossians 2:20–23, 3:7–10
2 Timothy 2:11–13
Revelation 3:4

YOUR THOUGHTS

SPIRITUAL CLOTHING
AND GOD'S PROVISION

"God will provide" is very difficult to remember when life gets out of our control, especially when we are extremely invested such as worrying about loved ones or our future. We need to blanket ourselves in reading our Bibles, praying, talking with other Christians, and recalling the times in our own pasts when God came through for us supernaturally. These spiritual activities will ease our hearts and minds at such times. Jesus didn't say it would be easy, but that he would be with us (Matthew 28:20).

Zechariah 3:3–5
Matthew 6:25–34
Luke 12:22–31
2 Corinthians 5:1–5
Ephesians 5:10–17
Revelation 3:4–5

YOUR THOUGHTS

CIRCUMSTANCES

The Bible gives help to believers in bad circumstances. It is sad that many people only turn to the finite wisdom of other people. While the thoughts and comfort of other people are truly gifts from God, the "final answer" to the questions of life comes directly from God.

Psalm 91:15, 118:5–9, 119:49–52
Matthew 6:25–34, 28:20
John 14:1–3, 25–27
Romans 8:28, 35, 37–40
Philippians 4:19
1 Thessalonians 5:16–18
Hebrews 2:14–18
1 Peter 1:3–9

YOUR THOUGHTS

_____

_____

_____

_____

_____

_____

_____

_____

_____

_____

_____

_____

_____

_____

_____

_____

_____

_____

_____

_____

_____

_____

SHARING IN CHRIST'S SUFFERINGS

Believers will experience everything from not fitting in to outright persecution, as did Jesus. While never to the degree he endured, we can offer these dark times in our lives to God as a sacrifice, as an opportunity to share in Christ's sufferings (Romans 8:17). God will not only empower us to stand strong but will also bless us with new life, just as he did for Jesus (Philippians 3:10). See *Bible Themes* for "Obedience/Empowerment" and "Circumstances."

Psalm 119:49–50
Matthew 10:37–39, 16:24, 20:22–23
Mark 8:34–35
John 15:18–21
Acts 14:19–22
Romans 8:12–17
2 Corinthians 1:3–5
Philippians 1:29–30, 3:10
1 Thessalonians 3:1–4
2 Timothy 1:8–12, 2:1–10, 3:12
Hebrews 10:32–39, 13:11–14
1 Peter 3:12–17, 4:12–19

YOUR THOUGHTS

PASSING THROUGH/ CITIZENS OF HEAVEN

As Christians, we can depend upon God to help us live in his will in a world where we frequently don't fit in (Philippians 3:20, 4:13). Followers of Jesus are different in ways not always appreciated, if not disdained by others. God will cover us with his protection, although it will always take much courage to "walk the walk" and a strong belief that pleasing God matters more than pleasing people.

John 15:18–19, 17:13–19
Romans 12:2
Ephesians 2:19
Philippians 3:17–21
Hebrews 11:8–16, 13:14
1 Peter 2:11–12
1 John 2:15–17

YOUR THOUGHTS

WORSHIP/SACRIFICE

True worship requires that we give ourselves to God to the fullest extent that we are able. He knows when we are giving him our all and when we are holding back.

Exodus 25:1–2
Psalm 40:6–8, 51:16–17, 116:17
Hosea 6:6
Matthew 6:7, 9:13, 12:7, 23, 25:40
John 4:23–24
Romans 12:1–2
Hebrews 13:15–16
James 2:14–26

YOUR THOUGHTS

GOD DOES NOT ACCEPT MINDLESS, RITUALISTIC ACTIVITIES AS SACRIFICES, OR EVEN WORSE, PRETENTIOUS PIETY (ISAIAH 29:13, MATTHEW 23:28)

Proverbs 15:8
Isaiah 1:13–20, 29:13
Matthew 12:7 (Jesus quotes Hosea 6:6), 23:23, 27–28
2 Corinthians 9:12
Hebrews 10:5–7 (Jesus quotes Psalm 40:6–8), 13:15–16

YOUR THOUGHTS

WORKS

Our own "works" not only cannot save us, but they must be motivated by a heart that cannot help but serve God. We understand his unmerited love and his great gift of salvation through the "work" of his son, Jesus Christ (1 John 4:10). No other motivation is acceptable to him. Only authentic faith produces good deeds unselfishly. As James teaches, this is living faith. We are saved by grace, and as new creations, God's love flows through us to others. Jesus said, "The King replied, 'I tell you the truth, whatever you did for one of the least of these brothers of mine, you did for me'" (Matthew 25:40).

Psalm 116:12, 16–17
Jeremiah 2:22
Hosea 6:6
Matthew 19:25–26, 25:40
John 12:26
Acts 26:20
Ephesians 2:8–10
Hebrews 13:15–16
James 2:14–26
1 John 4:9–12
Revelation 1:5–6

YOUR THOUGHTS

_____

_____

_____

_____

_____

_____

_____

_____

_____

_____

_____

_____

_____

_____

_____

_____

_____

_____

_____

_____

_____

_____

CALL

Sometimes God moves our hearts toward a particular service for his purpose. This is God "calling" us. Two great Bible role models for us are Abraham and Paul. If we look around us, hopefully, we will see many others.

Genesis 12:1–5
Exodus 36:2
Acts 9:1–22
Romans 1:1
1 Corinthians 1:1
Colossians 1:24–29
2 Timothy 1:11–12

YOUR THOUGHTS

HERE I AM, LORD

The response of the faithful servant of God is in each of the following verses. I love this response to God's call so much that I wrote it down every time I came across it for years and years. I believe that this was the beginning of my putting pencil to paper and writing *Mom's Bible Notes,* from which *Bible Themes* originated. How do we answer when God calls us?

Genesis 22:1 (Abraham to God)
Genesis 31:11 (Jacob to the angel of God)
Genesis 46:2 (Jacob to God)
Exodus 3:4 (Moses to God)
1 Samuel 3:4–6, 8, 16 (Samuel to God, thinking it was Eli)
Psalm 40:6–8 (David to God)
Isaiah 6:8 (Isaiah to God)
Isaiah 8:18 (Isaiah to God)
Acts 9:10 (New American Standard Version): "Behold I am here, Lord" (the disciple Ananias to God)
Hebrews 2:13 (Jesus quotes Isaiah 8:18)
Hebrews 10:7, 9 (Paul quotes Psalm 40:7–8)

YOUR THOUGHTS

OBEDIENCE/
EMPOWERMENT

God empowers believers who live in obedience to him to navigate through this life far better than we could ever do on our own. See *Bible Themes* for "Circumstances" and "Sharing in Christ's Sufferings."

Exodus 36:2

1 Samuel 18:12

1 Kings 8:58–61

1 Chronicles 29:19

Jeremiah 1:4–10, 17–19

Daniel 1:8–17

Micah 3:8

Habakkuk 3:19

Haggai 1:12-14

Zechariah 4:6–8

Luke 9:1, 6

John 14:10–12

1 Corinthians 12:1–4

Colossians 1:25, 29

1 Thessalonians 1:4–10, 2:13, 4:7–8

2 Timothy 1:8–14, 4:17

Titus 2:11–14

Hebrews 13:20–21

1 Peter 4:11

2 Peter 1:3

YOUR THOUGHTS

THE BATTLE IS THE LORD'S

There are times when only the power of God brings victories (1 Samuel 17:47).

Genesis 35:5
Exodus 14:13–14, 25, 23:27
Deuteronomy 1:29–31, 3:22, 9:1–3, 20:4
Joshua 3:7–17, 4:21–24, 10:42, 11:20, 23:3, 10
Judges 7:15–22
1 Samuel 7:10, 14:20, 17:47 (Here is it is plain English: "The battle is the Lord's.")
2 Samuel 5:22–25
1 Kings 20:28–30
2 Kings 6:17–18, 7:5–7, 19:35
1 Chronicles 14:15–16, 17:7–8
2 Chronicles 14:11–13, 17:10, 20:15–17, 24, 32:7–8, 20–22
Isaiah 31:8
Zechariah 9:12–16, 14:3–9
Luke 12:11–12, 21:15

YOUR THOUGHTS

NOTHING IS IMPOSSIBLE
WITH GOD (LUKE 1:37)

Genesis 18:14
Numbers 11:23
Jeremiah 32:17, 27
Matthew 19:26
Mark 10:27: "All things are possible with God."
Luke 1:37, 18:27

YOUR THOUGHTS

THE BODY: CHRIST THE HEAD/WE THE MEMBERS

Believers are joined to Christ and to each other (Romans 12:5, 1 Corinthians 6:17).

Romans 12:4–8
1 Corinthians 6:17, 12:1–7
Philippians 2:19–21
Colossians 2:9–10

YOUR THOUGHTS

_____
_____
_____
_____
_____
_____
_____
_____
_____
_____
_____
_____
_____
_____
_____
_____
_____
_____
_____
_____
_____
_____
_____

WE MIGHT BE THE ONLY
JESUS THEY EVER SEE

This is a quote from a speaker at the Bowery Mission in New York City, New York.

Psalm 119:74
Proverbs 4:18
2 Corinthians 6:3–10, 13:5
Philippians 1:12–14
1 Thessalonians 1:2–10
1 Timothy 4:15–16
1 Peter 2:12

YOUR THOUGHTS

JESUS RETURNING LIKE A THIEF IN THE NIGHT (1 THESSALONIANS 5:2)

We are to have our spiritual lives in order. When Jesus returns, as he promised, we don't want to be caught thinking, *Gee, someday I really have to look into this Jesus thing.* We are told to be ready. He might not come back for a thousand years, but then again, what if he comes tomorrow? Will we be ready?

Zechariah 14:7
Matthew 24:36–44, 25:1–13
Mark 13:32–37
Luke 21:32–36
1 Thessalonians 5:1–6
2 Peter 3:8–17
Revelation 3:3

YOUR THOUGHTS

Printed in the United States
by Baker & Taylor Publisher Services